THE PATH TO SUCCESS

The Path to Success

UNLOCKING YOUR MINDS FULL POTENTIAL

James Hewitt

Mind Your Success Coaching LLC.

Endorcements

I'm Grateful for James Hewitt. He has been an inspiration in my life over the years. His mindset coaching is life-changing. His coaching has helped me change not only my mindset but how I Perceive myself daily. His coaching has helped me stay true to myself, which has changed my life. His Knowledge, understanding, and wisdom have allowed me to remove negative barriers that have held me back.

Temika McCanns

Transformational Coach, Author of Becoming an Incredible Woman

The book Path to Success helped me to shift my mindset and help me look at challenges in life from a different perspective. Things can appear as mountains in your life, but knowing how to approach the mountains makes all the difference.

Brenda J. Williams

Author of Breakdown to Breakthrough: Breaking the Chains of Mental Bondage

Contents

1

Understanding the Success of Mindset

THE POWER OF THE MIND

This chapter will explore the incredible influence our minds have on achieving success. By understanding the power of our thoughts and beliefs, we can cultivate a success mindset that enables us to overcome challenges, reach our goals, and unlock our true potential.

Belief Systems: Our beliefs are the foundation of our mindset. They shape our perception of the world and determine what we believe to be possible or impossible. Examining and reshaping our limiting beliefs allows us to expand our horizons and open ourselves up to new opportunities and possibilities.

Positive Thinking: Positive thinking is vital in cultivating a successful mindset. By focusing on the positive aspects of situations and maintaining an optimistic outlook, we can overcome obstacles and

2 | JAMES HEWITT

setbacks more effectively. The power of positive thinking lies in its ability to attract positive experiences and outcomes into our lives.

Visualization and Affirmations: Visualization and affirmations are powerful tools that help us align our thoughts and beliefs with our desired outcomes. By vividly imagining our goals and affirming positive statements about ourselves and our abilities, we can reprogram our subconscious mind to support our success.

Mindfulness and Self-awareness: Mindfulness and self-awareness are essential to a successful mindset. By practicing mindfulness, we can become aware of our thoughts and emotions, allowing us to respond consciously rather than reactively. Self-awareness helps us identify self-limiting patterns and beliefs, enabling us to make positive changes.

The Power of Focus: To achieve success, it is crucial to maintain focus and concentration on our goals. We can channel our mental energy toward what truly matters by eliminating distractions and prioritizing tasks. The power of focus allows us to stay committed, make progress, and achieve remarkable results.

The power of the mind is truly extraordinary. By harnessing its potential through a success mindset, we can overcome obstacles, achieve our goals, and create a life of abundance and fulfillment. By embracing the concepts discussed in this subchapter, you can unlock the true power of your mind and embark on the path to success. Remember, success begins within you, and your mind holds the key to unlocking your full potential.

Believing in Yourself

In the journey toward success, one of the most crucial traits to cultivate is a strong belief in oneself. Even the most talented individuals can fall short of their true potential without self-belief. "Believing in Yourself" delves into the power of Self-confidence and how it can shape our mindset toward achieving success.

We tap into a limitless reserve of inner strength and resilience when we believe in ourselves. This belief propels us forward, even in the face of challenges and setbacks. The key is recognizing that success starts from within and that our thoughts and beliefs profoundly impact our actions and outcomes.

We will explore practical strategies to foster self-belief and develop a success mindset. One of the first steps is to challenge and reframe our negative self-talk. Often, we are our own harshest critics, doubting our abilities and questioning our worth. By replacing self-doubt with affirmations and positive self-talk, we can gradually build a foundation of belief in ourselves.

Another powerful tool is visualization. By vividly imagining ourselves achieving our goals and experiencing success, we create a mental blueprint that guides our actions and choices. Visualization helps to reinforce our belief in our capabilities and strengthens our resolve to pursue our dreams.

Furthermore, surrounding ourselves with a supportive network of individuals who believe in us can make a world of difference. As social beings, we are influenced by the people we interact with. By seeking out mentors, coaches, and like-minded individuals who share our aspirations, we can tap into their wisdom and encouragement, boosting our self-belief in the process.

Lastly, we will emphasize the importance of celebrating small victories along the way. Each step forward, no matter how small, shows our progress and reinforces our belief in our ability to succeed. By acknowledging and celebrating these achievements, we build momentum and strengthen our faith in our potential to overcome even more significant challenges.

"Believing in Yourself" is an essential subchapter highlighting the significance of Self-confidence. in cultivating a success mindset. Through practical strategies like positive self-talk, visualization, building a supportive network, and celebrating small victories, people can unlock their mind's full potential and chart their path to success with an unwavering belief in themselves. Remember, success starts from within, and by believing in yourself, you are already one step closer to achieving your dreams.

Overcoming Limiting Beliefs

One of the most significant obstacles we face in the journey toward success is the limiting beliefs that hold us back. These beliefs are deeply ingrained in our minds and can prevent us from reaching our full potential. However, identifying and challenging these limiting beliefs can unlock our mind's full potential and pave the way to success.

Limiting beliefs are negative thoughts or beliefs about ourselves, our abilities, and the world around us. These beliefs often stem from past experiences, societal conditioning, or fear of failure.

They act as self-imposed barriers, preventing us from taking risks, pursuing our dreams, and achieving our goals.

To overcome limiting beliefs, we must first become aware of them. Take a moment to reflect on your thoughts and identify any negative beliefs that may be holding you back. Are you constantly doubting your abilities? Do you believe that success is only reserved for others? Recognizing these beliefs is the First step towards overcoming them.

Once identified, it is important to challenge these beliefs with positive and empowering thoughts. Replace thoughts like "I'm not good enough" with "I am capable of achieving anything I set my mind to." Surround yourself with positive affirmations and repeat them daily. You can gradually rewire your mind and break free from limiting beliefs by consistently reinforcing positive thoughts.

Another effective strategy is to seek evidence that contradicts your limiting beliefs. For example, if you believe you are not good at public speaking, remind yourself of times when you successfully delivered a presentation or received positive feedback. This evidence will help you realize that your belief is not based on reality and can be overcome.

Additionally, surrounding yourself with a supportive community is crucial. Connect with like-minded individuals who have a success mindset and are on a similar journey. Share your challenges, fears, and victories with them. They can guide and inspire and hold you accountable for overcoming limiting beliefs.

Remember, overcoming limiting beliefs is a continuous process. It requires patience, persistence, and a commitment to personal growth. As you challenge and replace these limiting beliefs, you will begin to unlock your mind's full potential and open doors to new opportunities.

In conclusion, the path to success starts with overcoming limiting beliefs. By recognizing, challenging, and replacing these beliefs, we can break free from self-imposed barriers and unleash our true potential. With a success mindset, we can pave the way to achieving our goals and living a fulfilling life. Embrace the journey of personal growth and watch as your dreams become a reality.

Cultivating a Positive Attitude

In our journey toward success, our attitude is one of the most crucial factors that can significantly impact our outcomes. A positive attitude is like a magnet that attracts opportunities, helps overcome obstacles, and fuels our determination to reach our goals. The key unlocks our mind's full potential and sets us on the path to success.

A positive attitude is not something we are born with; it is a skill that can be cultivated and developed over time. It requires conscious effort and a commitment to self-improvement. So, how can we cultivate a positive attitude?

First and foremost, becoming aware of our thoughts and emotions is essential. We must vigilantly monitor our inner dialogue and identify any negative or self-limiting beliefs holding us back. By acknowledging these negative thoughts, we can challenge them and replace them with positive affirmations. This process of self-reflection allows us to rewire our minds and create a more positive outlook.

Another powerful method to cultivate a positive attitude is by practicing gratitude. Gratitude shifts our focus from what is lacking in our lives to what we already have. It allows us to appreciate small victories, acknowledge our strengths, and find joy in the present moment. By incorporating a daily gratitude practice into our lives, we train our minds to see the positive aspects of every situation.

Surrounding ourselves with positive influences is also crucial for developing a successful mindset. The company we keep greatly impacts our attitude and mindset. Therefore, we must surround ourselves with individuals who uplift and inspire us. Engaging in positive conversations, reading motivational books, and listening to uplifting podcasts are all ways to cultivate a positive attitude through external influences.

Lastly, we must remember that setbacks and failures are inevitable in the journey toward success. Instead of letting them discourage us, we should view them as opportunities for growth. Maintaining a positive attitude during challenging times allows us to learn from our mistakes, adjust our strategies, and persevere toward our goals.

Cultivating a positive attitude is not always easy, but it is a habit worth developing. By consciously choosing positivity, practicing gratitude, surrounding ourselves with positive influences, and embracing setbacks as learning opportunities, we can unlock our mind's full potential and create a success mindset.

In conclusion, the journey toward success begins with cultivating a positive attitude. This subchapter has explored the importance of self-reflection, gratitude, positive influences, and resilience in developing a positive mindset. By incorporating these practices into our lives, we can unlock our mind's full potential and pave the way for success. Remember, success starts with a positive attitude. Setting Clear Goals In order to achieve success and unlock your mind's full potential, one of the most important factors to consider is setting clear goals. Staying focused, motivated, and on track toward achieving your desired outcomes becomes difficult without clear goals. Setting clear goals provides a roadmap, guiding you through the steps required to reach your destination.

Setting Clear Goals

One of the most important factors to consider is setting clear goals to achieve success and unlock your mind's full potential. Staying focused, motivated, and on track toward achieving your desired outcomes becomes difficult without clear goals. Setting clear goals provides a roadmap, guiding you through the steps required to reach your destination.

When setting goals, it is crucial to be specific and precise. Vague goals such as "I want to be successful" or "I want to make more money" lack clarity and can lead to confusion and lack of direction. Instead, clearly define what success means to you and what specific achievements you need to accomplish to consider yourself successful. For instance, if success means starting your own business, set clear and measurable goals such as "I will launch my own business within the next six months" or "I will increase my business revenue by 20% within the next year."

Moreover, setting clear goals helps to prioritize your actions and allocate your resources effectively. By clearly identifying what needs to be done, you can avoid wasting time and energy on tasks that do not contribute to your ultimate success. Setting goals also provides a sense of purpose and motivation, as you have something concrete to work towards and measure your progress against.

It is important to note that goals should be challenging yet attainable. Setting goals that are too easy may not provide the motivation to propel you forward, while setting goals that are too unrealistic may lead to frustration and disappointment. Find a balance that stretches your abilities and pushes you out of your comfort zone while still being achievable with effort and dedication.

In addition, it is beneficial to break down your larger goals into smaller, manageable tasks or milestones. This allows you to track your progress and celebrate small victories along the way. Breaking down your goals also helps to prevent overwhelm, as you can focus on one step at a time rather than feeling overwhelmed by the enormity of the entire plan.

In conclusion, setting clear goals is essential to cultivating a success mindset. By being specific, precise, and realistic in setting your goals, you can provide yourself with a clear roadmap to success. Remember to break down your goals into smaller tasks, stay focused, and remain dedicated to achieving your desired outcomes. With clear goals in place, you will be well on your way to unlocking your mind's full potential and achieving your desired success.

Notes

2

Developing A Growth Mindset

Embracing Challenges

In the journey toward success, challenges are inevitable. They are the stepping stones that push us out of our comfort zones and propel us toward growth. By embracing these challenges, we develop a success mindset, unlocking our mind's full potential.

The path to success is not smooth; it is filled with obstacles, setbacks, and failures. However, we can rise above and learn valuable lessons in these moments. Embracing challenges means stepping up to face and conquer them head-on rather than shying away or giving up.

One of the key aspects of embracing challenges is developing a positive attitude. Instead of viewing challenges as roadblocks, we can see them as opportunities for personal and professional growth.

Embracing challenges allows us to overcome self-doubt and build resilience, which are vital traits for success.

When faced with a challenge, it is important to approach it with an open mind. Rather than fearing the unknown, we can view challenges as platforms for innovation and creativity. Embracing challenges encourages us to think outside the box and find innovative solutions, ultimately leading to personal and professional breakthroughs.

Another crucial element in embracing challenges is perseverance. Success is not achieved overnight; it requires dedication and persistence. Challenges test our perseverance and determination, pushing us to keep going even when the going gets tough. By embracing challenges and persisting through them, we develop the mental toughness necessary for success.

Furthermore, embracing challenges allows us to redefine our limitations. Often, we underestimate our abilities and settle for mediocrity. However, when faced with challenges, we must stretch our limits and discover our true potential. Embracing challenges helps us break free from self-imposed limitations and reach new heights of success.

In conclusion, embracing challenges is an essential mindset for success. We unlock our mind's full potential by viewing challenges as opportunities for growth, approaching them with a positive attitude, maintaining perseverance, and redefining our limitations. Embracing challenges allows us to overcome obstacles, develop resilience, and cultivate a success mindset to propel us toward our goals. So, let us embrace challenges with open arms and embark on the path to success.

Learning from Failure

Failure is often seen as a setback, a roadblock on the path to success. However, failure holds valuable lessons that can propel us toward achieving our full potential. In this subchapter, we will explore the concept of learning from failure and how it contributes to developing a success mindset.

One of the key aspects of a success mindset is the ability to view failure as an opportunity for growth rather than a reflection of personal inadequacy. Adults with a success mindset understand that failure is not the end but a stepping stone toward success. They embrace failure as a necessary part of the journey, knowing it provides valuable insights and lessons to drive them closer to their goals.

Learning from failure requires a shift in perspective. Instead of dwelling on the negative emotions that failure can evoke, successful individuals focus on the lessons learned from their mistakes. They analyze what went wrong, identify the factors that contributed to the failure, and devise strategies to avoid repeating those mistakes in the future. By doing so, they transform failure into a powerful learning experience that propels them forward.

Furthermore, a success mindset encourages adults to adopt a growth mindset. This means believing their abilities and intelligence can be developed through dedication and hard work. By embracing a growth mindset, individuals understand that failure is not a rejection of their inherent abilities but rather an indication of areas where they can improve. They view failure as an opportunity to expand their knowledge, skills, and capabilities, ultimately leading to greater success.

Learning from failure also involves resilience and perseverance. Adults with a success mindset understand that failure is not a permanent state but rather a temporary setback. They bounce back from failure by staying committed to their goals and adapting their strategies as needed. They understand that failure is often a necessary part of the journey toward success and are determined to persist despite obstacles.

In conclusion, learning from failure is crucial to developing a success mindset. Adults who embrace failure as an opportunity for growth, adopt a growth mindset, and demonstrate resilience and perseverance, are better equipped to unlock their mind's full potential. By viewing failure as a stepping stone towards success and extracting valuable lessons from their mistakes, they pave the way for personal and professional growth.

Embracing Continuous Learning

In today's fast-paced and ever-evolving world, success is no longer a destination but a journey. We must embrace continuous learning to unlock our mind's full potential. This subchapter delves into the significance of adopting a success mindset through lifelong learning and its transformative impact on personal and professional growth.

As adults, we often become complacent in our knowledge and skills, sticking to what we already know and rarely venturing outside our comfort zones. However, the world is constantly evolving, and to stay relevant and succeed, we must cultivate a mindset of continuous learning. This means being open to new ideas, seeking new knowledge, and constantly challenging ourselves to grow.

Embracing continuous learning is not only about gaining new knowledge but also about developing a growth mindset. This mindset allows us to see failures as opportunities for growth, embrace challenges as stepping stones to success, and persist in the face of adversity. By adopting a growth mindset, we can overcome our limitations, tap into our full potential, and achieve levels of success we never thought possible.

Lifelong learning is not limited to formal education or acquiring degrees; it encompasses a wide range of experiences and opportunities for growth. It can involve reading books, attending seminars and workshops, seeking mentors, exploring new hobbies, or engaging in meaningful conversations with like-minded individuals. Every interaction and experience has the potential to teach us something new and expand our horizons.

Embracing continuous learning also requires a commitment to self-reflection and self-improvement. It means being open to feedback, recognizing our strengths and weaknesses, and actively working on personal and professional development. By constantly striving to improve ourselves, we can enhance our skills, broaden our perspectives, and ultimately achieve greater success.

When we embrace continuous learning, it will be fundamental in developing our success mindset. By adopting a growth mindset, seeking out new knowledge and experiences, and committing to self-improvement, we can unlock our mind's full potential and achieve the success we desire. In this rapidly changing world, the path to success lies in our ability to adapt, learn, and grow. So, let us embrace the journey of continuous learning and unlock the limitless possibilities that await us.

Seeking Feedback and Growth Opportunities

One of the critical elements to developing a success mindset is the willingness to seek feedback and embrace growth opportunities. In order to unlock your mind's full potential, it is crucial to approach life with a growth mindset, which means being open to learning, improvement, and constructive criticism.

Feedback is a powerful tool that can provide valuable insights and help you identify areas for improvement. Whether it is from mentors, colleagues, or loved ones, seeking feedback allows you to gain a different perspective and see blind spots that you may have missed. It takes courage and humility to ask for feedback, but doing so can propel you forward on your path to success.

When seeking feedback, it is important to approach it with an open mind. Remember that feedback is not a personal attack but an opportunity for growth. Be open to constructive criticism and focus on using it to improve yourself. Instead of being defensive, ask questions and seek clarification to understand the feedback fully. Use it as a chance to reflect on your strengths and weaknesses and make necessary adjustments to reach your goals.

Additionally, growth opportunities can come in various forms. They can be found in challenging projects at work, pursuing new hobbies, or engaging in personal development activities. Embracing these opportunities allows you to stretch your abilities and expand your comfort zone. You can reach your mind's full potential by pushing past your limits.

When faced with growth opportunities, it is important to approach them with a positive mindset. Embrace challenges as chances for personal growth and learning. Even if you encounter setbacks or failures, view them as stepping stones toward success. Remember that success is not linear, and setbacks are often part of the journey. Learn from them, adapt, and keep moving forward.

In conclusion, seeking feedback and embracing growth opportunities are essential to developing a success mindset. You can gain valuable insights and make necessary improvements by being open to feedback. Embracing growth opportunities allows you to expand your abilities and reach new levels of success. Remember, success is not a destination but a continuous journey of self-improvement. So, be open-minded, embrace challenges, and unlock your mind's full potential.

Adopting a Solution-Oriented Approach

In order to achieve success in any aspect of life, whether it is in our careers, relationships, or personal goals, it is crucial to develop a solution-oriented mindset. This mindset lets us focus on finding solutions to challenges and obstacles rather than dwelling on problems. Adopting a solution-oriented approach can unlock our mind's full potential and pave the path to success.

One of the key aspects of a solution-oriented approach is shifting our mindset from a problem-focused perspective to a solution-focused one. Instead of getting stuck in a cycle of complaints and negativity, we train ourselves to look for opportunities and possibilities. This shift in perspective allows us to see challenges as stepping stones rather than roadblocks, empowering us to take action and find creative solutions.

Another critical aspect of a solution-oriented approach is taking personal responsibility for our circumstances. Rather than blaming external factors or other people for our failures or setbacks, we acknowledge that we have control over our responses and actions. By taking ownership of our choices, we can proactively seek solutions and make the necessary changes to achieve success.

Furthermore, cultivating a solution-oriented approach requires us to develop problem-solving skills. This involves breaking down complex challenges into smaller, manageable tasks, brainstorming potential solutions, and evaluating the pros and cons of each option. We can identify the most effective and efficient solutions to overcome obstacles and achieve our goals by thinking critically and analytically.

In addition, a solution-oriented approach also involves fostering a growth mindset. This means embracing a belief that our abilities and intelligence are not fixed but can be developed through effort and perseverance. With a growth mindset, we view setbacks and failures as opportunities for learning and growth rather than indicators of our limitations. This mindset allows us to bounce back from setbacks and strive for success.

In conclusion, adopting a solution-oriented approach is essential for cultivating a success mindset. By shifting our perspective, taking personal responsibility, developing problem-solving skills, and fostering a growth mindset, we can unlock our mind's full potential and overcome any obstacles that come our way. With this approach, we empower ourselves to take control of our success and create a fulfilling and prosperous life.

Notes

3

Cultivating Resilience and Perseverance

Understanding Resilience

Resilience is a fundamental trait crucial to success in every aspect of life. It is the ability to bounce back from setbacks, adapt to challenging situations, and maintain a positive mindset despite adversity. In this subchapter, we will delve deeper into the meaning of resilience and explore its significance in cultivating a success mindset.

Resilience is not innate but a skill that can be learned and developed over time. It is the driving force behind individuals who never give up, embrace failures as learning opportunities, and are determined to overcome obstacles on their path to success.

One key aspect of understanding resilience is recognizing that setbacks and failures are inevitable in any journey toward success.

They are not roadblocks but stepping stones providing valuable insights and lessons. Resilient individuals view challenges as opportunities for growth and use setbacks as fuel to propel themselves forward.

Another crucial factor in understanding resilience is the ability to adapt to change. Life is unpredictable, and success requires the flexibility to adjust to new circumstances. Resilient individuals possess a growth mindset, which allows them to embrace change, learn from it, and adapt their strategies accordingly. They understand that setbacks and unexpected events are not permanent but temporary hurdles that can be overcome with the right mindset and actions.

Moreover, resilience involves managing emotions and maintaining a positive outlook, even in adversity. It is about staying calm and composed during challenging times, focusing on solutions rather than dwelling on problems. Resilient individuals practice self-care, engage in positive self-talk, and surround themselves with a supportive network that encourages growth.

Understanding resilience is vital for cultivating a success mindset. Individuals can overcome self-doubt, fear of failure, and negative self-talk by developing resilience. Resilience empowers individuals to take risks, embrace challenges, and persist in facing obstacles. It fosters a belief in one's abilities and the confidence to pursue ambitious goals.

In conclusion, resilience is a key attribute for success, regardless of the endeavors one pursues. By understanding and cultivating resilience, individuals can navigate the ups and downs of life with grace and determination. Resilience enables individuals to persevere, learn from failures, adapt to change, and maintain a positive mindset throughout their journey toward success. Embracing resilience is the path to unlocking your mind's full potential and achieving the success you desire.

Building Emotional Resilience Emotional resilience is vital in today's fast-paced and competitive world. It is the ability to bounce back from setbacks, adapt to change, and maintain a positive outlook in the face of challenges. Strong emotional resilience is crucial for maintaining a success mindset in pursuing success.

The journey toward success is not always smooth, and setbacks are inevitable. However, you can learn to navigate these obstacles with grace and determination by cultivating emotional resilience.

One of the first steps toward building emotional resilience is developing self-awareness. Understanding your emotions and how they impact your thoughts and actions is essential. By acknowledging and accepting your feelings, you can begin to build a strong foundation of emotional resilience.

Next, it is crucial to develop healthy coping mechanisms. Stress and adversity are part of life, but how we respond to them determines our level of emotional resilience. Learning effective stress management techniques, such as deep breathing exercises or mindfulness meditation, can help you stay calm and focused during challenging times.

Another key aspect of building emotional resilience is cultivating a positive mindset. Positive thinking has a direct impact on our emotional well-being. By reframing negative thoughts and focusing on the positive aspects of a situation, you can build resilience and maintain a success mindset.

Developing Mental Toughness

In our fast-paced and highly competitive world, having a success mindset is crucial for achieving our goals and unlocking our full potential. One of the key components of a success mindset is developing mental toughness. Mental toughness is the ability to persevere and maintain focus in facing challenges, setbacks, and adversity. It is what separates those who achieve their dreams from those who give up when the going gets tough.

Building mental toughness does not happen overnight; it requires consistent effort and practice. Here are some strategies to help you develop mental toughness and cultivate a success mindset:

1. Embrace Challenges: Instead of avoiding difficult situations, embrace them as opportunities for growth. Challenges provide a chance to develop resilience and learn valuable lessons. You can build mental toughness by reframing challenges as stepping stones to success.

2. Set Clear Goals: Clarify your goals and break them down into smaller, manageable tasks. Setting clear goals helps you stay focused and motivated, even when faced with obstacles. Write down your goals and create an action plan to ensure you're making progress towards them.

3. Adopt a Positive Mindset: Cultivate a positive attitude and focus on solutions rather than problems. Train your mind to see setbacks as temporary and learn from them. Surround yourself with positive and supportive people who inspire and motivate you on your journey to success.

4. Practice Self-Discipline: Develop self-discipline by setting and sticking to routines. This will help you stay on track and avoid distractions. Learn to manage your time effectively and prioritize tasks that align with your goals.

5. Build Resilience: Resilience is the ability to bounce back from adversity. Accept that setbacks and failures are a part of the journey toward success. Learn from your failures, adapt, and keep moving forward. Cultivating resilience will strengthen your mental toughness.

6. Develop a Growth Mindset: Embrace a growth mindset, believing that your abilities and intelligence can be developed through dedication and hard work. See challenges as opportunities for growth and improvement rather than limitations.

Remember, developing mental toughness is a lifelong journey. It takes time and consistent effort to build a success mindset. By embracing challenges, setting clear goals, adopting a positive mindset, practicing self-discipline, building resilience, and developing a growth mindset, you can unlock your mind's full potential and achieve the success you desire. Stay focused, stay determined, and never give up on your dreams.

Staying Motivated during Difficult Times

In the journey toward success, there are bound to be difficult times that test our determination and resilience. Our mindset and ability to stay motivated become crucial during these challenging moments. In this "Staying Motivated During Difficult Times," we will explore powerful strategies and techniques to help you stay motivated during difficult times, ensuring that you continue to succeed.

1. Embrace the Power of Positive Thinking: A success mindset begins with cultivating a positive outlook. Train your mind to focus on solutions rather than problems, and reframe setbacks as opportunities for growth. Maintaining a positive mindset will help find the strength to stay motivated even when faced with adversity.

2. Set Clear and Attainable Goals: Goals provide a sense of direction and purpose, which is essential during difficult times. Break down your larger goals into smaller, manageable tasks that you can achieve daily or weekly. Celebrate each milestone and use them as fuel to keep pushing forward.

3. Seek Support: Surround yourself with a network of like-minded individuals who can provide encouragement and support. Join communities or groups that share your goals and values, as they can offer valuable insights and motivation during challenging times.

4. Practice Self-Care: Taking care of yourself physically, mentally, and emotionally is vital for maintaining motivation. Make time for activities that rejuvenate you, such as exercise, meditation, or hobbies. Ensure you get enough rest, eat well, and stay hydrated. A healthy and balanced lifestyle contributes significantly to your overall motivation and well-being.

5. Learn from Failure: Failure is not the end but an opportunity to learn and grow. Instead of dwelling on past mistakes, embrace them as valuable lessons and adjust your approach accordingly.

Remember that every successful person has encountered failure at some point, and it is through perseverance and the willingness to learn that they have achieved their goals.

6. Visualize Success: Visualization is a powerful tool that can keep you motivated even in the face of adversity. Take a few moments each day to visualize yourself achieving your goals and experiencing the success you desire. This mental exercise will reinforce your motivation and keep your focus aligned with your aspirations.

Remember, difficult times are temporary, and your success mindset will guide you through them. By adopting these strategies and techniques, you can stay motivated, overcome challenges, and unlock your mind's full potential on the path to success.

Overcoming Obstacles and Staying Persistent

In the journey toward success, obstacles are inevitable. They can range from personal limitations to external challenges that seem insurmountable. However, what separates those who achieve greatness from those who fall short is their ability to overcome these obstacles and stay persistent.

One key aspect of developing a success mindset is understanding that obstacles are not roadblocks but opportunities for growth. Instead of viewing them as setbacks, successful individuals see obstacles as stepping stones toward their goals. They recognize that each challenge presents a chance to learn, adapt, and become stronger.

To overcome obstacles effectively, it is crucial to develop resilience. Resilience is the ability to bounce back from failures and setbacks to persevere in the face of adversity. It involves maintaining a positive attitude, staying focused on the end goal, and refusing to give up. Individuals can maintain their motivation by cultivating resilience even when faced with insurmountable obstacles.

Another important aspect of overcoming obstacles is developing problem-solving skills. A success mindset requires individuals to approach challenges with a solution-oriented mindset. Instead of dwelling on the problem, successful individuals actively seek solutions and explore strategies to overcome the obstacle. They are unafraid to think outside the box and seek help or guidance when needed.

Furthermore, staying persistent is crucial for long-term success. Many people give up when faced with initial setbacks or obstacles. However, success rarely comes easily or quickly. It requires dedication, patience, and a commitment to keep going even when progress seems slow. Staying persistent means maintaining focus on the end goal, even when faced with distractions or temporary setbacks.

A success mindset also involves understanding the power of perseverance. Recognizing that setbacks and failures are not indicators of personal worth or ability is important. Instead, they are opportunities for growth and self-improvement. By persevering through challenges, individuals gain valuable experience, learn valuable lessons, and develop the skills necessary for success.

In conclusion, overcoming obstacles and staying persistent are essential to developing a success mindset. By viewing obstacles as opportunities for growth, cultivating resilience, developing problem-solving skills, and staying persistent, individuals can overcome any challenge that comes their way. Remember, success is not a destination but a journey, and the ability to overcome obstacles is what propels individuals toward their goals and unlocks their mind's full potential.

Notes

4

Harnessing the Power of Visualization and Affirmations

The Science Behind Visualization

Visualization is a powerful mental technique that involves creating vivid mental images of desired outcomes. It has long been used by successful individuals across various fields, from athletes to entrepreneurs, as a tool to unlock the mind's full potential.

Scientists have discovered that when we visualize an action or outcome, the same neural pathways in our brain are activated as when we actually perform that action. This phenomenon, known as "mental rehearsal," has been extensively studied and proven to enhance performance and improve overall mindset.

The brain is a complex organ that constantly interprets and responds to the information it receives. When we visualize ourselves achieving a goal, our brain perceives it as a real experience, triggering a series of positive psychological and physiological responses. This process strengthens the connection between our brain and our desired outcome, making it more likely to become a reality.

Visualization also helps to rewire our subconscious mind. Our subconscious mind is responsible for our beliefs, habits, and behaviors, often operating on autopilot. By engaging in regular visualization exercises, we can overwrite limiting beliefs and replace them with empowering ones. This rewiring allows us to develop a growth mindset, fostering resilience, creativity, and a can-do attitude.

Furthermore, visualization activates our brain's reticular activating system (RAS). The RAS acts as a filter, prioritizing information based on what we focus on. By visualizing our goals and desires, we program our RAS to seek opportunities and resources aligning with our visions. This heightened awareness allows us to notice and seize opportunities that may have previously gone unnoticed.

Numerous studies have demonstrated the effectiveness of visualization in achieving success. For example, athletes who mentally rehearse their performances consistently outperform those who solely rely on physical practice. Similarly, entrepreneurs who visualize the steps needed to accomplish their business goals are more likely to succeed.

In conclusion, visualization is not just a fancy technique; it has a solid scientific basis. By practicing visualization regularly, we can tap into the power of our minds, reprogram our subconscious, and align our actions with our desired outcomes. Whether you aim to excel in sports, business, or personal growth, harnessing the science behind visualization can unlock your mind's full potential and set you on the path to success.

Creating Powerful Mental Imagery

In the pursuit of success, one of the most powerful tools we possess is our mind. Our thoughts and beliefs shape our reality, and harnessing the power of mental imagery can significantly transform our mindset and propel us toward achieving our goals.

Visualizing success is a technique that has been utilized by countless successful individuals throughout history. By creating vivid mental images of our desired outcomes, we tap into the immense power of the subconscious mind.

It is essential to understand that mental imagery is not limited to visual perception alone. It encompasses all our senses - sight, sound, touch, taste, and smell. Engaging multiple senses in our mental imagery creates a more profound and realistic experience that imprints our subconscious.

The first step in creating powerful mental imagery is clearly defining your goals. What is it that you want to achieve? Be specific and detailed in your visualization. Imagine every aspect of your success, from the sights and sounds surrounding it to the emotions you would feel when you attain it.

Next, find a quiet, comfortable space to relax and focus solely on your visualization. Close your eyes and take several deep breaths, allowing yourself to enter a state of deep relaxation. As you begin to visualize, imagine yourself already living your desired outcome. See yourself engaging in the activities that represent your success. Hear the sounds associated with your achievements. Feel the emotions of joy, fulfillment, and accomplishment coursing through your mind and body.

Repetition is key to reinforcing the power of mental imagery. Incorporate daily visualization exercises into your routine. Spend at least 10 to 15 minutes each day immersing yourself in your mental imagery. The more you engage with your visualization, the more your subconscious mind accepts it as your reality.

Lastly, it is essential to maintain a positive mindset throughout the process. Believe in your ability to achieve your goals and trust that your visualization is guiding you toward success. Embrace gratitude for the progress you make along the way, as this will further strengthen your success mindset.

Creating powerful mental imagery is crucial in developing a success mindset. By harnessing the power of our thoughts and engaging our senses, we can shape our reality and propel ourselves toward achieving our goals. Dedicate time daily to visualize your success, and watch as your mindset transforms, unlocking your mind's full potential.

Practicing Affirmations for Success

One key aspect often overlooked in the journey to success is the power of affirmations. Affirmations are positive statements that we repeat to ourselves to shift our mindset and unlock our mind's full potential. By consistently practicing affirmations, we can cultivate a success mindset that empowers us to overcome challenges and achieve our goals.

Affirmations rewire our subconscious mind, significantly shaping our thoughts, emotions, and actions. When we repeat positive affirmations, we effectively reprogram our minds to focus on success, abundance, and possibilities.

One of the most important steps in practicing affirmations is to choose the right ones that resonate with our goals and aspirations. For example, if our goal is to become financially independent, we can affirm statements such as "I am deserving of financial abundance" or "Money grows effortlessly into my life." By repeating these affirmations daily, we begin to believe in our potential to achieve financial success.

Consistency is key when it comes to practicing affirmations. Making it a daily ritual is essential, ideally at the start of each day. Doing so sets a positive tone for the day ahead and aligns our thoughts with success. Affirmations can be repeated silently or spoken aloud, whichever feels more comfortable and authentic.

To enhance the effectiveness of affirmations, it is beneficial to engage our senses. Visualizing ourselves already achieving our goals while repeating affirmations can profoundly impact our subconscious mind. By vividly picturing our success and feeling its associated emotions, we reinforce the belief that success is not only possible but inevitable.

Furthermore, affirmations can complement additional practices such as meditation, journaling, or visualization exercises. These techniques create a holistic approach to developing a success mind-set and reinforce the positive affirmations we repeat.

It is important to note that practicing affirmations requires patience and perseverance. While the effects may not be immediate, we can gradually reprogram our minds to embrace success and unlock our full potential with consistent practice.

In conclusion, practicing affirmations for success is a powerful tool in cultivating a success mindset. By choosing the right afPrmations, being consistent in our practice, engaging our senses, and complementing afPrmations with other techniques, we can rewire our subconscious mind and unlock our mind's full potential. So, let us start each day with positive affirmations and embrace the journey toward success with confidence and determination.

Integrating Visualization and Affirmations into Daily Routine

In the pursuit of success, having the right mindset is crucial. Our thoughts and beliefs shape our actions and ultimately determine the outcomes we achieve in life. To unlock our mind's full potential and pave the path to success, we must embrace powerful tools such as visualization and affirmations. Integrating these practices into our daily routine allows us to transform our mindset and align ourselves with success.

Visualization is a technique that involves creating vivid mental images of our desired goals and outcomes. By visualizing ourselves already achieving our goals, we tap into the power of our subconscious mind and program it to work towards manifesting our desires. When we consistently visualize our goals, we create a clear picture of what we want to achieve, which energizes and motivates us to take action. By visualizing success, we build the belief that we can achieve our goals, which becomes the driving force behind our actions.

Affirmations, on the other hand, are positive statements that we repeat to ourselves consistently. By affirming what we want to achieve, we rewire our subconscious mind and replace negative self-talk with empowering beliefs. AfPrmations help us cultivate a success mindset by instilling confidence, self-belief, and resilience. When we repeat affirmations daily, we condition our minds to focus on our strengths, opportunities, and potential for growth. This positive mindset becomes the foundation for our actions and decisions, leading us closer to success.

Integrating visualization and affirmations into our daily routine requires consistency and commitment. Start by setting aside a few minutes each day for these practices. Find a quiet and comfortable space where you can relax and focus. Begin by visualizing your goals, imagining every detail and sensation associated with achieving them. Feel the emotions of success, and let them fuel your motivation.

Next, incorporate affirmations into your routine. Create a list of positive statements that resonate with your goals and values. Repeat these affirmations to yourself, silently or aloud, with conviction and belief. Visualize the affirmations becoming your reality and embrace the positive energy they bring.

To enhance the effectiveness of these practices, consider using visual aids such as vision boards or written affirmations displayed in prominent places. Surround yourself with images and words that remind you of your goals and affirm your success.

By integrating visualization and affirmations into your daily routine, you will gradually rewire your mind for success. As you consistently focus on your goals and affirm your capabilities, you will notice a shift in your mindset and a newfound confidence in your ability to achieve anything you set your mind to. Embrace these powerful practices, and unlock your mind's full potential on the path to success.

Utilizing Visualization for Goal Achievement

Visualization is a powerful tool to unlock your mind's full potential and assist you on the path to success. By harnessing the power of your imagination, you can create a clear and vivid picture of your goals and aspirations, making them more tangible and attainable. In order to achieve success, it is crucial to have a clear vision of what you want to accomplish. Visualization allows you to create a mental image of your desired outcome, enabling you to focus your energy and efforts toward achieving it. By visualizing your goals, you are essentially programming your mind for success.

One of the key benefits of visualization is that it helps to align your conscious and subconscious mind. Your conscious mind sets the goals, but your subconscious drives your actions and behaviors. By consistently visualizing your goals, you send a clear message to your subconscious, reinforcing your commitment and increasing your motivation to achieve them.

Visualization can also help you overcome obstacles and setbacks along your journey to success. By mentally rehearsing challenging situations, you can prepare yourself for potential roadblocks and develop strategies to overcome them. Seeing yourself overcoming obstacles in your mind's eye will strengthen your belief in your ability to overcome them in reality.

To effectively utilize visualization for goal achievement, it is important to create a regular practice. Set aside dedicated time daily to visualize your goals, preferably in a quiet and peaceful environment. Close your eyes and imagine yourself already achieving your desired outcome. Engage all your senses to make the visualization as vivid and real as possible. See the details, hear the sounds, feel the emotions, and experience the joy of success.

Visualization is not a mere daydreaming exercise; it requires focus, intention, and belief. By consistently practicing visualization, you are reprogramming your mind for success, aligning your thoughts, emotions, and actions toward achieving your goals.

In conclusion, visualization is a powerful tool for individuals with a success mindset. By harnessing the power of your imagination, you can create a clear and vivid picture of your goals, align your conscious and subconscious mind, overcome obstacles, and increase your motivation and belief in your ability to succeed. Make visualization a regular practice in your journey to success and unlock your mind's full potential.

Notes

5

Mastering Self-Discipline and Time Management

UNDERSTANDING THE IMPORTANCE OF SELF-DISCIPLINE

In the journey towards success, self-discipline emerges as a crucial key. It is the foundation upon which a success mindset is built. This subchapter explores the significance of self-discipline and its transformative power in unlocking your mind's full potential. Self-discipline is the ability to control and regulate oneself to pursue long-term goals. It involves making conscious choices and taking actions that align with your objectives, even when faced with distractions, temptations, or setbacks. It requires commitment, perseverance, and a strong sense of personal responsibility.

One of the primary reasons self-discipline is essential for success is that it helps you stay focused. In today's fast-paced world, distractions are abundant. Without discipline, it's easy to get sidetracked by social media, endless emails, or other unproductive activities. By practicing self-discipline, you can prioritize your goals and allocate your time and energy toward them. This unwavering focus allows you to make consistent progress and achieve remarkable results.

Self-discipline also fosters self-mastery. When you are disciplined, you gain control over your thoughts, emotions, and actions. Instead of being driven by impulses or external circumstances, you become the captain of your own ship. This sense of control empowers you to make deliberate choices that align with your values and long-term vision. It enables you to overcome challenges, develop healthy habits, and make positive changes in your life.

Moreover, self-discipline cultivates resilience. Success is rarely linear; obstacles, failures, and setbacks often accompany it. In these moments, self-discipline is a shield, preventing you from giving up or becoming discouraged. It fuels your determination and provides the mental strength to bounce back from adversity. With self-discipline, you can embrace challenges as growth opportunities and continue moving toward your goals.

In conclusion, self-discipline is an invaluable asset on the path to success. It empowers you to stay focused amidst distractions, gain control over your thoughts and actions, and bounce back from setbacks. By cultivating self-discipline, you unlock your mind's full potential and pave the way for a success mindset. Embrace self-discipline as a guiding principle in your life, and witness its transformative power.

Developing Self-Control and Willpower

In the journey toward success, one crucial aspect that often separates the winners from the rest is the ability to develop self-control and willpower. These two powerful traits are like a guiding compass that steers individuals toward their goals, helping them overcome obstacles and stay focused on their path to success.

Self-control is the ability to regulate one's thoughts, emotions, and behaviors to achieve desired outcomes. It involves making conscious choices, resisting temptations, and staying committed to long-term goals. Conversely, willpower is the mental strength that enables individuals to persevere through challenges, setbacks, and distractions.

Developing self-control and willpower is not an innate talent but a skill that can be cultivated and strengthened over time. Just like physical muscles, the more you exercise and train your self-control and willpower, the stronger they become.

One effective way to enhance self-control and willpower is by practicing mindfulness and self-awareness. By becoming more aware of your thoughts, emotions, and behaviors, you can identify patterns hindering your progress and consciously try to change them. Mindfulness exercises like meditation and deep breathing can help calm the mind, reduce stress, and improve focus, ultimately increasing self-control and willpower.

Another strategy to develop self-control and willpower is to set clear and realistic goals. Breaking down big goals into smaller, manageable tasks makes them more achievable and allows you to measure your progress along the way. Celebrating these small victories will boost your motivation and reinforce your self-control and willpower.

Building a strong support system is equally important in developing self-control and willpower. Surrounding yourself with like-minded individuals who share your goals and aspirations can provide the encouragement, accountability, and guidance needed to stay on track. Engaging in regular discussions, attending workshops, or joining success-oriented communities can be immensely beneficial.

Lastly, taking care of your physical health is essential for developing self-control and willpower. A well-rested and nourished body is better equipped to handle challenges and make rational decisions. Getting enough sleep, eating a balanced diet, and engaging in regular exercise are proven ways to enhance your overall self-control and willpower.

By consciously working on developing self-control and willpower, you are unlocking your mind's full potential and setting yourself up for a successful and fulfilling life. Remember, success is not just about achieving external milestones; it is a journey of self-discovery and personal growth.

Creating Effective Daily Routines

In the pursuit of success, one of the most powerful tools at our disposal is the establishment of effective daily routines. A well-designed routine can transform our lives by guiding our actions, boosting productivity, and cultivating a success mindset.

By incorporating key habits into our daily lives, we can unlock our mind's full potential and pave the way for achieving our goals.

The First step in creating an effective daily routine is identifying our priorities. Ask yourself: What are the most important tasks and goals I want to accomplish? Focusing on our priorities ensures that our time and energy are directed toward activities that truly matter. This clarity of purpose is the foundation of a success mindset.

Once we have identified our priorities, allocating specific time slots for each task is crucial. Scheduling our activities helps us stay organized and ensures that we make progress toward our goals. Whether it's allocating time for creative work, exercise, or self-reflection, a well-planned routine allows us to make the most of our day.

In addition to scheduling, it is important to incorporate healthy habits into our daily routines. Taking care of our physical and mental well-being is essential for maintaining a success mindset. Regular exercise, meditation, and adequate sleep are just a few habits that can enhance our overall productivity and mental clarity. By investing in self-care, we are investing in our success.

Furthermore, it is vital to eliminate distractions and create an environment conducive to focus. In today's digital age, getting caught up in the constant influx of information and notifications is easy. To counteract this, we can establish designated periods of uninterrupted work and limit our exposure to distractions. We can enhance our productivity and concentration by creating a dedicated space for deep work.

Finally, it is important to review and adjust our daily routine regularly. Life is dynamic, and our priorities and circumstances may change over time. By regularly evaluating our routines, we can ensure that they align with our current goals and aspirations. Flexibility and adaptability are key to maintaining a success mindset.

In conclusion, creating effective daily routines is crucial for cultivating a success mindset. By identifying priorities, scheduling tasks, incorporating healthy habits, eliminating distractions, and regularly reviewing our routines, we can unlock our mind's full potential and pave the path to success. Remember, success is not a destination but a journey, and our daily routines are the stepping stones along the way.

Prioritizing Tasks and Managing Time Effectively

In today's fast-paced world, where time seems to slip through our fingers like sand, it is crucial to master the art of prioritizing tasks and managing time effectively. This subchapter aims to equip them with the tools and strategies to develop a successful mindset by maximizing their valuable time. The foundation of effective time management lies in setting clear goals and establishing priorities. Without a clear direction, getting overwhelmed and losing focus becomes easy. Begin by identifying and breaking your long-term goals into smaller, actionable tasks. You can tackle each task with purpose and intention, ultimately moving closer to your desired outcome.

One of the key principles for success is learning to differentiate between urgent and important tasks. Urgent tasks often demand immediate attention but may not necessarily contribute to your long-term goals. On the other hand, important tasks are aligned with your objectives and have a significant impact on your success. By prioritizing important tasks, you ensure that your time and energy are invested in activities that truly matter.

Creating a schedule or a to-do list is essential to manage your time effectively. This helps you visualize your day, allocate time for each task, and track your progress. Remember to be realistic with your time estimates, allowing for unexpected interruptions or delays. Additionally, consider using time management techniques such as the Pomodoro Technique, which involves working in focused bursts followed by short breaks. This method helps maintain productivity and prevents burnout.

While managing time is essential, it is equally crucial to manage your energy levels. Recognize when you are most productive and schedule your most challenging tasks during those peak times. Take regular breaks to recharge and engage in activities that promote relaxation and mental clarity, such as exercise or meditation.

Lastly, embrace the power of delegation and learn to say no. It is impossible to do everything alone; trying to do so only leads to burnout and inefficiency—delegate tasks others can do, allowing you to focus on high-priority responsibilities. Similarly, learn to say no to requests or activities that do not align with your goals or drain your time and energy.

By implementing these strategies and adopting a success mindset, you can unlock your mind's full potential and achieve remarkable results. Prioritizing tasks and managing time effectively increases productivity and success and allows for a better work-life balance.

Mastering these skills will empower you to overcome obstacles, seize opportunities, and pave your path to success.

Overcoming Procrastination and Distractions

In today's fast-paced and highly competitive world, developing a success mindset is crucial for achieving our goals and unlocking our mind's full potential. However, one common hurdle often stands in the way of success is procrastination and distractions. These two seemingly innocent roadblocks can derail our progress and prevent us from reaching our true potential. We will explore effective strategies and techniques to overcome procrastination and eliminate distractions, empowering you to stay focused and on track toward your goals.

Procrastination, the act of delaying or postponing tasks, can be detrimental to our success. It robs us of valuable time and hinders our ability to accomplish what we set out to do. To overcome procrastination, it is essential to understand its root causes and implement practical solutions. We will delve into the psychology behind procrastination, exploring why we tend to put off tasks and how to break free from this self-sabotaging habit. By recognizing our triggers and implementing time management techniques, we can regain control of our time and increase productivity.

Distractions, on the other hand, are constant temptations that divert our attention away from our goals. In our digital age, where smartphones and social media are ever-present, it is increasingly challenging to maintain focus. However, by implementing proven strategies, we can minimize distractions and create an environment conducive to success. We will explore techniques such as setting clear boundaries, creating a distraction-free workspace, and utilizing technology to our advantage. Incorporating these strategies into our daily lives allows us to cultivate laser-like focus and achieve remarkable results.

Additionally, we will discuss the importance of developing a success mindset as a foundation for overcoming procrastination and distractions. We can strengthen our determination and resilience by cultivating self-discipline, setting achievable goals, and maintaining a positive attitude. We will explore practical exercises and mindset shifts that will help you stay motivated and overcome any obstacles that come your way.

In conclusion, the path to success requires overcoming procrastination and distractions. By understanding the psychology behind these obstacles and implementing effective strategies, we can regain control of our time, eliminate distractions, and cultivate a success mindset. Armed with these powerful tools, you will be well-equipped to unlock your mind's full potential and achieve the success you desire. Now is the time to take action, break free from the chains of procrastination, and focus on what truly matters – your journey toward success.

Notes

6

Building Strong Relationships and Networks

THE POWER OF NETWORKING

In today's fast-paced and interconnected world, networking has become essential for success in any field. Whether you are an entrepreneur, a professional, or an aspiring individual, the ability to build and maintain strong relationships can significantly impact your journey toward achieving your goals. "The Power of Networking" gives a blueprint on how it can help you unlock your mind's full potential in your pursuit of success.

Networking is not merely about exchanging business cards or attending social events; it is about building meaningful connections with like-minded individuals who can support and inspire you along your path. Expanding your network opens doors to new opportunities, ideas, and resources that can propel you forward.

Surrounding yourself with successful and positive-minded people can significantly influence your mindset and motivate you to reach greater heights.

One key benefit of networking is the ability to gain valuable insights and knowledge from others who have already achieved what you aspire to. By engaging in conversations and sharing experiences, you can learn from their successes and failures, avoiding common pitfalls and accelerating your growth. In addition, networking provides a platform to seek advice, guidance, and mentorship from individuals who have walked a similar path and can offer valuable perspectives.

Furthermore, networking enables you to showcase your skills, expertise, and unique qualities to a wider audience. By actively participating in professional communities, industry events, and online platforms, you can establish yourself as a thought leader and gain visibility among your peers. This visibility enhances your brand and opens doors to potential collaborations, partnerships, and career advancement opportunities.

Networking is not limited to physical interactions; the digital age has expanded the scope of networking to online platforms and social media. Utilizing these platforms effectively can help you connect with individuals across the globe, breaking barriers of distance and expanding your reach. Engaging in online communities, sharing valuable content, and participating in discussions can enhance your online presence and attract like-minded individuals into your network.

In conclusion, networking is a powerful tool that can unlock your mind's full potential in your journey toward success. Building and nurturing meaningful relationships gives you access to knowledge, opportunities, and support that can accelerate your growth. Embrace networking as an integral part of your success mindset, and watch as it transforms your personal and professional life. Remember, success is not achieved in isolation; it results from the connections we forge and the relationships we cultivate.

Effective Communication Skills

In today's fast-paced and interconnected world, effective communication skills have become essential for success in every area of life. Whether it is in our relationships, professional careers, or even our self-expression, the ability to communicate effectively is a crucial skill that can unlock our mind's full potential.

Communication is not simply about speaking or writing; it is a dynamic process that involves active listening, understanding, and conveying messages clearly and concisely. By honing our communication skills, we can easily overcome obstacles, build stronger relationships, and achieve our goals.

To develop effective communication skills, it is important to start with active listening. Many of us often focus on our thoughts and opinions without truly hearing what others have to say. By actively listening, we can understand the perspectives and emotions of those around us, leading to better understanding and more meaningful interactions. Active listening involves maintaining eye contact, asking clarifying questions, and providing feedback to ensure the speaker feels heard and valued.

Another important aspect of effective communication is being mindful of our non-verbal cues. Our body language, facial expressions, and tone of voice significantly convey our message. By being aware of our nonverbal communication, we can ensure that our words align with our intentions, enhancing our message's impact.

Additionally, developing strong verbal communication skills is crucial. This includes using clear and concise language, avoiding jargon or technical terms when speaking to a non-expert audience, and being mindful of the tone and volume of our voice. It is important to remember that effective communication is a two-way street, so being open to feedback and adapting our communication style accordingly is essential for success.

Mastering effective communication skills improves our relationships and enhances our professional prospects. Employers value individuals who can articulate their thoughts, collaborate with diverse teams, and resolve conflicts effectively. Developing these skills allows us to stand out in a competitive job market and advance our careers.

In conclusion, effective communication skills are critical to the success mindset. We can unlock our mind's full potential by actively listening, being mindful of our non-verbal cues, and developing strong verbal communication skills. These skills enable us to build stronger relationships, navigate challenges, and confidently achieve our goals. Whether in our personal or professional lives, effective communication is the key to unlocking success and realizing our true potential.

Building Meaningful and Supportive Relationships

In our journey toward success, we often underestimate the power of building meaningful and supportive relationships. We tend to focus solely on our personal growth and development, forgetting that our connections with others are crucial in shaping our mindset and, ultimately, our success.

Humans are social beings, and our relationships influence our thoughts, emotions, and actions. Surrounding ourselves with individuals who share our success mindset can be a game-changer. These individuals understand our challenges, offer valuable insights, and push us to reach our full potential.

To build such relationships, we must first define what a success mindset means to us. Is it about achieving Financial stability, excelling in our careers, or finding fulfillment in our personal lives? Once we clearly understand our goals and aspirations, we can seek individuals aligning with our vision.

Networking events, conferences, and workshops focused on personal growth and success mindset are excellent places to meet like-minded individuals. Engage in conversations, exchange ideas, and be open to learning from others. Remember, building relationships is a two-way street. Offer support, encourage, and share your experiences to create a foundation of trust and mutual respect.

While it is beneficial to surround ourselves with individuals who share our success mindset, it is equally important to cultivate diverse relationships. People from different backgrounds, cultures, and perspectives can offer unique insights and broaden our horizons. Embrace diversity and seek out individuals who challenge your beliefs and push you outside your comfort zone.

Building meaningful and supportive relationships also requires active listening and empathy. Take the time to understand others' perspectives, show genuine interest in their lives, and offer your support when needed. Celebrate their successes and be there to lend a helping hand during challenging times. Remember, success is not a solo journey but a collective effort.

Lastly, building meaningful and supportive relationships also means setting healthy boundaries. Surround yourself with individuals who inspire and uplift you, and distance yourself from toxic relationships that drain your energy and hinder your growth. Choose your tribe wisely and create a positive and nurturing personal and professional development environment.

In conclusion, building meaningful and supportive relationships is an essential component of a success mindset. Surrounding ourselves with like-minded individuals who share our vision, embracing diversity, and cultivating empathy are key factors in unlocking our mind's full potential. Remember, success is not just about personal achievements; it is about the collective growth and support we offer each other on the path to success.

Nurturing Professional Connections

In today's fast-paced and interconnected world, the importance of nurturing professional connections cannot be overstated.

Building and maintaining a strong network of colleagues, mentors, and industry experts is crucial for individuals striving for success in their respective fields. This subchapter will explore the significance of professional connections, provide practical tips on how to forge and nurture them and highlight the positive impact they can have on one's success mindset.

First and foremost, professional connections serve as a valuable source of knowledge and expertise. By surrounding yourself with like-minded individuals who have already succeeded in their careers, you gain access to a wealth of information and insights. Whether it's learning about industry trends, exploring new opportunities, or seeking advice on challenges you may be facing, these connections can provide invaluable guidance and support.

Additionally, professional connections can open doors to new opportunities. Many career advancements and lucrative business deals are often a result of referrals and recommendations from trusted connections. By actively cultivating and maintaining relationships with professionals in your field, you increase your chances of being top of mind when opportunities arise. Remember, success is not solely determined by your efforts but also by the network of people you surround yourself with.

Furthermore, these connections can offer emotional support and motivation. The journey to success can be challenging, and having a strong support system of individuals who understand your ambitions and aspirations can make all the difference. Building relationships with like-minded professionals creates a community of individuals who can provide encouragement, share experiences, and offer guidance during difficult times. This emotional support can help you maintain a positive mindset and stay motivated on your path to success.

To nurture professional connections effectively, it is essential to prioritize quality over quantity. Instead of collecting a vast number of superficial connections, focus on building genuine relationships with individuals who share your values and goals. Engage in meaningful conversations, attend networking events, and utilize online platforms to stay connected and updated with your network.

In conclusion, nurturing professional connections is vital to developing a success mindset. These connections provide access to valuable knowledge, open doors to new opportunities, and offer emotional support. By actively investing time and effort into building and maintaining these relationships, individuals can enhance their chances of success in their careers and personal lives. Remember, success is not a solitary journey but one built upon the support and guidance of a strong professional network.

Leveraging Relationships for Success

In the journey toward success, it is important to recognize the power of relationships and their impact on our personal and professional growth. Whether in business, career advancement, or personal development, leveraging relationships can be a game-changer for those with a success mindset.

Success is not achieved in isolation; it requires collaboration, support, and guidance from others. Building strong and meaningful relationships can provide you with the necessary resources, knowledge, and opportunities to propel yourself forward.

One of the key aspects of leveraging relationships for success is networking. Networking is not just about attending events and collecting business cards; it is about forming genuine connections with like-minded individuals who can contribute to your growth. By building a network of professionals and mentors, you gain access to a wealth of knowledge and experience to help you navigate your path to success. Another important aspect is building a support system. Surrounding yourself with positive and supportive individuals who believe in your abilities can be a significant driving force. They can encourage, offer valuable advice, and hold you accountable for your goals. Your support system can be a group of friends, family members, or even a mastermind group of like-minded individuals who are also on their journey toward success.

Furthermore, it is crucial to foster mutually beneficial relationships. Instead of solely focusing on what others can do for you, approach relationships with a mindset of giving and adding value. By offering others your skills, knowledge, and resources, you create a reciprocal exchange where both parties can benefit and grow together. Leveraging relationships for success also involves seeking out mentors and role models. Mentors provide guidance, wisdom, and perspective to help you overcome obstacles and make informed decisions. They have already walked the path you aspire to tread, and their insights can save you time, effort, and potential mistakes. Success is not achieved in isolation but rather through the power of relationships. By networking, building a support system, fostering mutually beneficial relationships, and seeking out mentors, you can leverage these connections to unlock your mind's full potential and propel yourself toward success. Embrace the power of relationships and watch how they can transform your journey toward achieving your goals and living a successful life.

Notes

7

Embracing Change and Adaptability

ACCEPTING THE NEED FOR CHANGE

In our journey toward success, one of the most crucial steps we must take is accepting the need for change. Change is an inevitable part of life, essential for personal growth and achieving a success mindset. However, many adults find it challenging to embrace change due to fear, uncertainty, or being stuck in their comfort zones. Accepting the need for change and how it can unlock your mind's full potential is vital.

Change brings new opportunities, challenges, and experiences that push us out of our comfort zones. It forces us to adapt, learn, and grow, ultimately leading to personal and professional success. However, accepting the need for change requires a shift in mindset. It requires us to let go of old beliefs, patterns, and habits that no longer serve us. By doing so; we open ourselves up to endless possibilities and opportunities for growth.

One of the main reasons people resist change is fear. Fear of the unknown, fear of failure, and fear of stepping into unfamiliar territory. However, it is important to remember that fear is just an illusion, holding us back from reaching our true potential. When we embrace change, we confront our fears head-on, breaking through the barriers that prevent us from achieving success.

Another reason people struggle with change is a lack of clarity or direction. Change can be overwhelming if we don't have a clear vision or purpose. By reflecting on our goals and values, we can better align ourselves with the changes we must make. This clarity provides a sense of purpose and direction, making change more manageable and motivating.

Accepting the need for change also requires a willingness to let go of the past. It's easy to hold onto past mistakes, regrets, or failures, but doing so only hinders our progress. Instead, we must learn from our past experiences and use them as stepping stones toward a better future.

To embrace change, it is crucial to cultivate a growth mindset. A growth mindset acknowledges that dedication and hard work can develop abilities and intelligence. By adopting this mindset, we view challenges as opportunities for growth and see failures as stepping stones toward success.

In conclusion, accepting the need for change is essential to developing a success mindset. It requires us to overcome fear, gain clarity, and let go of the past. By embracing change, we open ourselves up to new possibilities, personal growth, and, ultimately, unlocking our mind's full potential. So, let go of the resistance and embrace change as a catalyst for success.

Developing a Flexible Mindset In the journey toward success, adapting and embracing change is crucial. A flexible mindset allows us to navigate life's challenges and uncertainties, enabling us to stay focused on our goals and achieve true success. This subchapter will explore the importance of developing a flexible mindset and provide practical strategies to help you cultivate this invaluable trait.

To begin, let's understand what a flexible mindset entails. It is the ability to think and respond to situations open-mindedly, adaptable, and resiliently. It involves embracing new ideas, perspectives, and experiences rather than clinging to rigid beliefs or fixed attitudes. A flexible mindset allows us to see obstacles as opportunities for growth and learning rather than insurmountable barriers.

One of the key benefits of a flexible mindset is its power to foster innovation and creativity. By embracing change, we open ourselves up to new possibilities and solutions that we may not have considered before. As adults seeking success, we must challenge our assumptions and continuously explore alternative approaches. A Flexible mindset allows us to think outside the box and find unique solutions to problems, giving us a competitive edge in our professional and personal lives.

Cultivating a flexible mindset requires consciously breaking free from our comfort zones. It involves developing a growth mindset, where we view failure as a stepping stone toward success and embrace the idea of continuous learning. By reframing setbacks as opportunities for growth, we can bounce back stronger, armed with newfound knowledge and resilience.

In addition, practicing mindfulness can greatly assist in developing a flexible mindset. Mindfulness allows us to be fully present in the moment, free from judgment and preconceived notions. This non-judgmental awareness enables us to approach situations with a fresh perspective, open to new possibilities and creative solutions.

Furthermore, surrounding ourselves with diverse perspectives and experiences can help us cultivate a flexible mindset. We expand our understanding and challenge our biases by seeking out different viewpoints. Engaging in meaningful conversations and seeking feedback from others can broaden our horizons and foster an environment of growth and learning.

Developing a flexible mindset is crucial for adults seeking success. It allows us to adapt to change, embrace new ideas, and approach challenges with resilience and creativity. By cultivating a growth mindset, practicing mindfulness, and seeking diverse perspectives, we can unlock our mind's full potential and pave the path to success. Remember, success is not a destination; it is a mindset.

Adjusting to New Situations and Challenges

One must be prepared to face many new situations and challenges in the journey toward success. Life is ever-changing, and adapting and adjusting is crucial for maintaining a success mindset. Embracing new situations and challenges provides practical strategies to help you navigate them confidently and resiliently.

Change is inevitable, and often, it is accompanied by uncertainty. However, successful individuals understand that new situations and challenges present opportunities for growth and learning. They approach these situations with a positive mindset, viewing them as stepping stones toward their ultimate goals. By shifting your perspective and embracing change, you open yourself up to endless possibilities and pave the way for personal and professional growth.

Developing a strong sense of self-awareness is vital to adjust to new situations and challenges. Understand your strengths, weaknesses, and triggers that might hinder your progress. Self-awareness empowers you to identify potential obstacles and develop strategies to overcome them. You can confidently face any new situation or challenge head-on by acknowledging your limitations and seeking improvement.

Maintaining a growth mindset is another key aspect of adjusting to new situations and challenges. Embrace the belief that your abilities and intelligence can be developed through dedication and hard work. This mindset allows you to approach challenges with curiosity and resilience, understanding that setbacks are temporary and serve as valuable learning opportunities. By reframing failure as a stepping stone toward success, you will build the resilience necessary to adapt to any situation.

Effective communication and collaboration are also essential when faced with new situations and challenges. Seek guidance and support from mentors or peers who have experience in similar situations. Surround yourself with a strong support network that encourages you to explore new possibilities and helps you stay motivated during challenging times. Collaboration provides diverse perspectives and fosters a sense of belonging and shared purpose.

Adjusting to new situations and challenges is integral to the path to success. By embracing change, developing self-awareness, maintaining a growth mindset, and fostering effective communication and collaboration, you can navigate through any obstacle that comes your way. Remember, success is not solely determined by external circumstances but rather by your ability to adapt and thrive in the face of adversity. So, embrace new situations and challenges, and unlock your mind's full potential on the path to success.

Embracing Innovation and Continuous Improvement

In today's fast-paced world, embracing innovation and continuous improvement is essential for achieving success and unlocking your mind's full potential. This subchapter will explore the importance of adopting a success mindset that embraces change, welcomes new ideas, and constantly seeks improvement.

To begin with, it is crucial to understand that success is not a destination but a continuous journey. Those with a success mindset understand there is always room for growth and improvement. They actively seek out new opportunities and are open to exploring innovative ideas. By embracing innovation, they stay ahead of the curve and adapt quickly to changing circumstances.

Innovation is the driving force behind progress and improvement. It enables us to challenge the status quo and think outside the box. When we embrace innovation, we become more adaptable and resilient, which is critical for success in today's rapidly evolving world. By continually seeking new ways of doing things, we can find more efficient and effective solutions to problems and achieve greater results.

Continuous improvement is another key aspect of a success mindset. It involves a commitment to constantly learning and developing oneself. As adults, we must recognize that there is always something new to learn and skills to acquire. By embracing continuous improvement, we can enhance our knowledge, sharpen our skills, and stay relevant in our chosen fields.

One way to foster a success mindset is by cultivating a culture of learning and curiosity. We should proactively seek new knowledge and experiences through reading books, attending seminars, enrolling in courses, or engaging in meaningful conversations with others. Exposing ourselves to diverse perspectives and ideas expands our thinking and challenges our preconceived notions.

Moreover, it is crucial to be open to feedback and constructive criticism. Embracing innovation and continuous improvement requires us to be receptive to new ideas and willing to adapt our approaches. By actively seeking feedback from mentors, peers, and even subordinates, we can identify areas for improvement and make the necessary adjustments to achieve our goals.

In conclusion, embracing innovation and continuous improvement is vital for cultivating a success mindset. By adopting a forward-thinking approach, seeking out new ideas, and constantly striving for personal growth, we can unlock our mind's full potential and achieve extraordinary success in all areas of our lives. Let us embrace change, challenge ourselves, and be open to new possibilities. The path to success begins with a mindset that embraces innovation and continuous improvement. Thriving in a Dynamic and Ever-Changing World In today's fast-paced and constantly evolving world, the key to success lies in our ability to adapt and thrive in the face of change. The path to success is no longer a linear trajectory but a journey through a dynamic and ever-changing landscape. To navigate this terrain successfully, we must cultivate a success mindset that embraces change and harnesses the power of our mind's full potential.

A success mindset is about embracing a growth mindset, recognizing that our abilities and intelligence can be developed through dedication and hard work. This mindset allows us to view challenges and setbacks as opportunities for growth and learning rather than roadblocks to success. With a success mindset, we can overcome any obstacles that come our way and continue to move forward in our personal and professional lives.

One of the critical aspects of thriving in a dynamic world is the ability to adapt to change. Change is not something to be feared but rather embraced as an opportunity for growth and innovation. By developing a success mindset, we can train ourselves to be reliable and adaptable in the face of change, enabling us to seize new opportunities and confidently navigate uncertain times.

Another important element of thriving in a dynamic world is the ability to think critically and creatively. Success is no longer just about having knowledge and skills; it's about being able to apply them in unique and innovative ways. By unlocking our mind's full potential, we can tap into our creative thinking and problem-solving abilities, enabling us to develop new and innovative solutions to our challenges.

Furthermore, thriving in a dynamic world requires continuous learning and self-improvement. The success mindset encourages us to seek new knowledge and skills and stay curious and open-minded. By continuously learning and adapting, we can stay ahead of the curve and ensure our success in an ever-changing world.

To thrive in a dynamic and ever-changing world, we must cultivate a success mindset that embraces change, adaptability, critical thinking, and continuous learning. By unlocking our mind's full potential, we can confidently navigate uncertain times, seize new opportunities, and set ourselves up for success in all areas of our lives. Embrace the challenges, stay open-minded, and let your success mindset guide you on the path to success.

Notes

8

Cultivating a Growth-Oriented Environment

SURROUNDING YOURSELF WITH POSITIVE INFLUENCES

In our journey towards success, the company we keep plays a significant role in shaping our mindset and determining our outcome. It is said that we are the average of the five people we spend the most time with. Therefore, it is crucial to surround ourselves with positive influences to propel us toward achieving our goals.

Positive influences can come in various forms, such as friends, mentors, colleagues, or virtual communities. These individuals possess qualities that inspire and motivate us to reach higher levels of success. They radiate optimism, perseverance, and a growth mindset. Interacting with such individuals stimulates our creativity, fuels our determination, and instills in us the belief that success is attainable.

One of the key benefits of surrounding ourselves with positive influences is the power of collective wisdom. When we engage with people who have already achieved success in our desired niche, we gain access to their knowledge, experience, and insights. Their guidance can save us from making costly mistakes and fast-track our progress toward our goals. By observing their habits and adopting their mindset, we can learn valuable lessons that will shape our path to success.

Moreover, positive influences can elevate our self-belief and confidence. When surrounded by individuals who believe in our abilities and encourage us to push our limits, we are more likely to overcome self-doubt and take bold steps toward our goals. Their unwavering support becomes a constant reminder that we are capable of achieving greatness.

However, it is essential to choose our influences wisely. Negative influences can drain our energy, hinder our progress, and impede our success. They might be individuals who constantly criticize our ideas, discourage our ambitions, or bring us down with their pessimism. To maintain a success mindset, it is crucial to distance ourselves from such influences and seek out individuals who uplift and inspire us.

Surrounding ourselves with positive influences is not only beneficial for our personal growth but also for our overall well-being. It creates a supportive network that fosters collaboration, motivation, and accountability. By cultivating a circle of positive influences, we create an environment that nurtures our success mindset and propels us toward unlocking our mind's full potential.

In conclusion, the path to success is paved with the company we keep. Surrounding ourselves with positive influences is essential for developing and maintaining a success mindset. By choosing individuals who inspire, motivate, and guide us, we create an environment that fosters growth, cultivates belief in our abilities, and propels us toward achieving our goals. Remember, your success is greatly influenced by the people you surround yourself with, so choose wisely.

Creating a Supportive Network

In our journey toward success, one crucial aspect often overlooked is building a supportive network. Surrounding ourselves with like-minded individuals who share our passion for success can profoundly impact our mindset and, ultimately, our achievements. This subchapter will delve into the significance of creating a supportive network and provide practical tips on cultivating such relationships.

A supportive network can be instrumental in developing and maintaining a success mindset. Connecting with individuals with similar goals and aspirations opens us to a wealth of knowledge, experience, and encouragement. Being part of a supportive network allows us to learn from others' successes and failures, providing valuable insights and lessons to accelerate our journey toward success. Moreover, a supportive network is a constant source of motivation and inspiration. Surrounding ourselves with individuals who are driven and determined can be contagious. Their energy and enthusiasm can help us stay focused, motivated, and committed to our goals. When we see others achieving their dreams, it reaffirms our belief in our abilities and reminds us that success is within our reach.

Building a supportive network starts with identifying individuals with similar values and goals. Seek networking events, conferences, or online communities catering to your niche. Engage in conversations, ask questions, and share your own experiences. By actively participating in these communities, you can build meaningful relationships with like-minded individuals who can become part of your support system.

Furthermore, it's essential to nurture these relationships by offering support and encouragement to others. Success is not a zero-sum game, and by uplifting and empowering others, we create a positive ecosystem where everyone can thrive. Celebrate the successes of your network and offer assistance when needed. Being a supportive ally will attract individuals who reciprocate that support and contribute to your growth.

Remember, success is not achieved in isolation. By creating a supportive network, we surround ourselves with individuals who believe in us, challenge us, and propel us toward greatness. So, invest time and effort into building and nurturing these relationships. Together, we can unlock our mind's full potential and embark on the path to success.

Participating in Personal Development Programs

Personal growth and self-improvement have become essential to success in today's fast-paced world. To unlock our mind's full potential, engaging in personal development programs is crucial. These programs provide a structured framework for individuals to cultivate a success mindset and achieve their goals. This subchapter will explore why participating in personal development programs is essential for adults seeking to enhance their success mindset.

1. Identifying and Overcoming Limiting Beliefs: Personal development programs help individuals identify and address their limiting beliefs. These programs provide tools and techniques to challenge negative thought patterns and replace them with empowering beliefs. By participating in such programs, adults can break free from self-imposed limitations and develop a success mindset that fuels their ambitions.

2. Goal Setting and Action Planning: Participating in personal development programs teaches individuals to set clear, attainable goals and create action plans to achieve them. These programs provide practical strategies to break big goals into smaller, manageable steps. By learning effective goal-setting techniques, adults can develop a success mindset that enables them to stay focused, motivated, and accountable for their actions.

3. Developing Emotional Intelligence: Emotional intelligence plays a significant role in personal and professional success. Personal development programs offer various tools and exercises to enhance emotional intelligence. By developing self-awareness, empathy, and effective communication skills, adults can easily navigate

challenging situations, build strong relationships, and cultivate a success mindset that fosters personal growth.

4. Building Resilience and Overcoming Obstacles: Success is not without its share of challenges and setbacks. Personal development programs equip individuals with the skills to handle adversity and build resilience. By participating in these programs, adults learn to view obstacles as opportunities for growth, develop problem-solving skills, and cultivate a success mindset that persists despite adversity.

5. Networking and Collaboration: Personal development programs often provide opportunities for networking and collaboration with like-minded individuals. By connecting with others on the same journey, adults can exchange ideas, gain support, and expand their network. Collaborative efforts foster a success mindset by creating a supportive community that encourages growth and provides valuable resources and insights.

Participating in personal development programs is instrumental in cultivating a success mindset. These programs empower adults to overcome limiting beliefs, set goals, enhance emotional intelligence, build resilience, and foster collaboration. By actively engaging in personal development, individuals can unlock their mind's full potential and embark on the path to success. Remember, personal growth is a lifelong journey, and participating in personal development programs is a significant step towards achieving your goals and living a fulfilling life.

Seeking Mentors and Coaches

In the journey toward success, it is essential to recognize the importance of seeking mentors and coaches. These individuals play a crucial role in unlocking our mind's full potential and nurturing a success mindset. Whether you are an aspiring entrepreneur, a professional looking to advance in your career, or someone seeking personal growth, having mentors and coaches can make a significant difference in your path to success.

Mentors are experienced individuals who have already achieved what we aspire to accomplish. They provide guidance, support, and wisdom based on their own experiences. A mentor can offer valuable insights, help us avoid common pitfalls, and provide a fresh perspective on our goals and aspirations. They act as a guiding light, steering us toward the right path and keeping us focused on our objectives.

Coaches, on the other hand, are professionals trained to unlock our full potential. They possess the skills and knowledge to help us identify our strengths and weaknesses, set achievable goals, and develop strategies to overcome obstacles. Coaches provide accountability, support, and motivation, ensuring we stay committed to our journey toward success. They challenge us to push our limits, break through self-imposed barriers, and strive for excellence.

Seeking mentors and coaches is not a sign of weakness or incompetence but rather a demonstration of our commitment to personal and professional growth. These individuals have walked the path we aspire to follow, and their guidance can save us precious time and energy. They can provide invaluable advice, share their networks, and open doors that would otherwise remain closed. Mentors and coaches act as a source of inspiration, reminding us of what is possible and helping us believe in our potential.

Defining our goals and aspirations is crucial to finding the right mentor or coach. Identifying someone who has already achieved what we desire will ensure that their guidance aligns with our vision. Networking events, professional organizations, and online platforms dedicated to mentorship and coaching are excellent avenues to connect with potential mentors and coaches.

Remember, success is not a solo journey. It is a collaborative effort that requires the support and guidance of those who have already walked the path. By seeking mentors and coaches, we can tap into their wisdom, learn from their experiences, and accelerate our journey toward success. So, take the first step and unlock your mind's full potential with the guidance and support of mentors and coaches.

Fostering a Growth Mindset Culture in Organizations

Organizations must adapt and grow to stay competitive in today's fast-paced and ever-evolving world. One key factor determining an organization's success is its culture. A growth mindset culture is a powerful tool that can propel organizations to new heights, fostering innovation, continuous learning, and overall success.

So, what exactly is a growth mindset? It is the belief that abilities and intelligence can be developed through dedication, hard work, and perseverance. Unlike a fixed mindset, where individuals believe their abilities are static, a growth mindset allows people to embrace challenges, learn from failures, and constantly strive for improvement.

Why is fostering a growth mindset culture crucial for organizations? Firstly, it promotes a culture of learning and development. When employees believe their efforts and dedication can lead to personal and professional growth, they become motivated to improve their skills and knowledge continuously. This, in turn, benefits the organization as it becomes more innovative and adaptable.

Secondly, a growth mindset culture encourages resilience and perseverance. In a rapidly changing world, organizations face numerous challenges and setbacks. However, employees with a growth mindset view setbacks as opportunities for growth and learning rather than insurmountable obstacles. This resilience allows organizations to overcome challenges and bounce back stronger than before.

Additionally, a growth mindset culture fosters collaboration and teamwork. When individuals believe in their ability to grow and develop, they become more open to feedback and constructive criticism. This creates an environment where employees can openly share ideas, learn from one another, and work together towards common goals, ultimately driving success for the organization.

Creating a growth mindset culture requires deliberate effort from leaders and managers. It starts with promoting a learning-oriented environment, where mistakes are viewed as opportunities for growth rather than something to be punished. Encouraging employees to set challenging goals, providing regular feedback and recognition, and offering opportunities for skill development are all crucial in fostering a growth mindset culture.

In conclusion, fostering a growth mindset culture in organizations is essential for success in today's rapidly changing world. By embracing the belief that abilities can be developed through dedication and hard work, organizations can create an environment that promotes learning, resilience, collaboration, and innovation. Leaders and managers play a vital role in cultivating this culture, and by doing so, they unlock the full potential of their employees and propel their organizations toward greater success.

Notes

9

Overcoming Fear and Taking Calculated Risks

IDENTIFYING AND UNDERSTANDING FEAR

Fear is a universal emotion that can profoundly impact our lives. It can hold us back from reaching our full potential and hinder our progress toward success. In order to overcome fear and cultivate a success mindset, it is crucial first to identify and understand the various forms fear can take.

Fear can manifest in different ways for different individuals. It can be triggered by past traumas, a fear of failure, or even the fear of the unknown. Understanding the root cause of our fears is the First step towards conquering them. By delving deep into our emotions and past experiences, we can gain valuable insights into our fears and begin to dismantle them.

One of the most common fears adults face is the fear of failure. This fear often stems from societal expectations or personal insecurities. However, it is important to recognize that failure is not inherently negative. In fact, it is through failure that we learn and grow the most. By reframing our perspective on failure and embracing it as a stepping stone toward success, we can overcome this fear and move forward with confidence.

Another form of fear that often plagues adults is the fear of the unknown. Stepping out of our comfort zones and into unfamiliar territory can be intimidating. However, in these moments of uncertainty, we have the greatest potential for growth. By acknowledging and accepting the fear of the unknown, we can develop a mindset that embraces change and embraces new opportunities.

Understanding our fears is not enough; we must also learn how to manage and overcome them. This involves developing strategies to cope with fear when it arises. Techniques such as deep breathing, visualization, and positive affirmations can help calm our minds and reframe our thoughts. Additionally, seeking support from mentors or joining a community of like-minded individuals can provide valuable guidance and encouragement.

In conclusion, fear is a natural part of the human experience, but it should not be allowed to define our path to success. By identifying and understanding our fears, we can take the necessary steps to overcome them and cultivate a success mindset. Embracing failure as a learning opportunity and embracing the unknown as an opportunity for growth are crucial steps toward unlocking our mind's full potential. With determination, resilience, and support, we can conquer our fears and pave the way for a successful and fulfilling life.

Challenging Limiting Beliefs and Anxieties

One of the biggest obstacles adults often face in pursuing success is their own limiting beliefs and anxieties. These negative thoughts and fears can keep us from reaching our full potential and achieving our goals. However, by challenging these beliefs and anxieties, we can unlock our mind's full potential and cultivate a success mindset.

Limiting beliefs are the thoughts and beliefs we hold about ourselves and our abilities that hinder our progress. They often stem from past experiences, negative self-talk, or societal conditioning. These beliefs create a fixed mindset that tells us we are incapable of achieving our goals or not deserving of success. To challenge these beliefs, we must first identify them and recognize how they hold us back.

On the other hand, anxieties are the fears and worries that prevent us from taking risks and stepping out of our comfort zone. They can paralyze us with self-doubt and prevent us from seizing opportunities. To overcome anxieties, we must confront them head-on and take small steps toward facing our fears.

One effective strategy for challenging limiting beliefs and anxieties is through reframing our thoughts. Instead of viewing challenges as obstacles, we can see them as opportunities for growth and learning. By shifting our perspective, we can transform our beliefs and anxieties into empowering thoughts that fuel our motivation and drive for success.

Another powerful tool is visualization. By visualizing ourselves successfully overcoming obstacles and achieving our goals, we can reprogram our subconscious mind to believe in our abilities. Visualization helps us build confidence and strengthens our belief in ourselves, enabling us to break free from the chains of limiting beliefs and anxieties.

Furthermore, seeking support from like-minded individuals or a mentor who has already achieved success can be invaluable in challenging and overcoming limiting beliefs and anxieties. Surrounding ourselves with positive and supportive people who believe in our potential can boost our confidence and guide us toward success.

Challenging limited beliefs and anxieties is crucial for unlocking our mind's full potential and cultivating a success mindset. By reframing our thoughts, practicing visualization, and seeking support, we can break free from the shackles of self-doubt and fear and pave the way for unlimited success. Remember, success starts in the mind, and by challenging our beliefs and anxieties, we can create a mindset that propels us toward achieving our greatest aspirations.

Developing Courage and Resilience

In the journey toward success, courage, and resilience are the most important attributes to cultivate. These qualities empower individuals to face challenges head-on, overcome obstacles, and persevere in the face of adversity. This subchapter will explore how to develop these essential traits and unlock your mind's full potential. Courage is not the absence of fear but rather the ability to take action despite it. It is about facing your fears and pushing beyond your comfort zone. To develop courage, it is crucial to identify your fears and understand that they often stem from limiting beliefs or past experiences. By challenging these beliefs and reframing your mindset, you can start to build the courage necessary to pursue your goals.

One effective way to cultivate courage is through small, incremental steps. Start by setting small goals that take you slightly outside your comfort zone and gradually increase the difficulty as you build confidence. Celebrate each step forward, no matter how small, as it reinforces your courage and resilience.

Resilience, on the other hand, is the ability to bounce back from setbacks and disappointments. It is the mindset that embraces failures as opportunities for growth and learning. Resilient individuals understand that setbacks are not permanent but rather temporary roadblocks that can be overcome with determination and perseverance.

To develop resilience, it is essential to cultivate a positive mindset. Practice reframing negative thoughts into positive ones and focus on the lessons learned from each setback. Surround yourself with supportive individuals who encourage and guide you during challenging times. Additionally, engage in self-care activities such as exercise, meditation, or journaling to nurture your mental and emotional well-being.

Building courage and resilience is an ongoing process that requires consistent effort and commitment. Embrace challenges as opportunities for growth and view failures as stepping stones toward success. Developing these qualities will unlock your mind's full potential and cultivate a success mindset.

Remember, success is not measured solely by the outcome but also by the journey. It is the ability to face adversity, learn from failures, and keep moving forward. So, take a deep breath, believe in yourself, and embark on the path to success with courage and resilience.

Assessing Risks and Making Informed Decisions

In the journey toward success, assessing risks and making informed decisions is crucial to separating those who achieve their goals from those who falter. Developing a success mindset entails understanding the potential risks involved in any endeavor and having the confidence to make well-informed decisions based on careful evaluation.

To begin with, assessing risks involves identifying potential obstacles or challenges that may arise during the pursuit of success. This requires a realistic and objective analysis of the situation at hand. By recognizing potential pitfalls or setbacks, individuals can better prepare themselves to navigate them effectively. This step plays a vital role in minimizing potential losses and maximizing the chances of success.

Once risks have been identified, gathering as much relevant information as possible is essential to make informed decisions. Successful individuals are not afraid to seek out different perspectives, conduct thorough research, and consult with experts in their respective fields. By considering multiple sources of information, they can understand the risks involved and the possible outcomes of their choices. This knowledge empowers them to make decisions confidently, knowing they have considered all available options.

Furthermore, a success mindset involves embracing uncertainty and being open to taking calculated risks. While feeling apprehensive about the unknown is natural, successful individuals understand that great accomplishments often require stepping out of their comfort zones. They recognize that playing it safe may limit their potential for growth and innovation. By carefully weighing the potential rewards against the risks, they can make bold decisions that propel them toward their goals.

It is worth emphasizing that assessing risks and making informed decisions is not a one-time process. Successful individuals continuously evaluate and adapt their strategies as circumstances change and new challenges arise. They remain flexible and open-minded, ready to adjust their course whenever necessary. This ability to pivot and make informed decisions in the face of uncertainty is a hallmark of a success mindset.

In conclusion, developing a success mindset requires mastering the skill of assessing risks and making informed decisions. Individuals can confidently navigate their journeys toward success by objectively identifying potential obstacles, gathering relevant information, embracing uncertainty, and remaining adaptable. Remember, success is not solely determined by the absence of risks but rather by the ability to assess and overcome them.

Embracing Failure as a Learning Opportunity

In our journey toward success, failure is often seen as a setback or a signal of defeat. However, what if we view failure as an opportunity for growth and learning? This subchapter aims to shift your perspective and help you embrace failure as a stepping stone toward achieving a success mindset.

Failure is inevitable, and even the most successful individuals have faced their fair share of setbacks. The key lies in how we respond to these failures and what we learn from them. Instead of dwelling on the negative emotions and self-doubt that failure often brings, we can reframe our mindset and see it as a valuable lesson.

One of the most significant advantages of embracing failure is the opportunity to learn from our mistakes. By reflecting on what went wrong and understanding the factors that led to the failure, we can gain valuable insights and make necessary adjustments for future endeavors. Failure allows us to identify our weaknesses and work on improving them, ultimately leading us closer to success.

Furthermore, failure teaches us resilience and perseverance. When faced with a setback, developing a growth mindset and viewing failure as a temporary obstacle rather than an ultimate defeat is essential. By embracing failure, we become more resilient, learning to bounce back stronger and more determined than ever before. Each failure becomes a stepping stone toward achieving our goals as we gain the strength and perseverance to overcome future challenges.

Moreover, failure allows us to develop humility and empathy. When we experience failure ourselves, we gain a deeper under-standing of the struggles and challenges others face. This empathy strengthens our relationships and helps us become more supportive and compassionate in our interactions with others.

To embrace failure as a learning opportunity, letting go of the fear of failure is crucial. Fear can paralyze us, preventing us from taking risks and pursuing our dreams. By adopting a growth mindset and viewing failure as a natural part of the journey toward success, we can overcome our fears and unlock our mind's full potential.

In conclusion, failure should not be seen as a roadblock but as a stepping stone toward success. By embracing failure as a learning opportunity, we gain valuable insights, develop resilience, and cultivate empathy. Let go of the fear of failure and embrace it as an essential part of your journey toward unlocking your mind's full potential.

Notes

10

Sustaining Success and Embracing Growth

CELEBRATING ACHIEVEMENTS AND MILESTONES

In the journey toward success, it is crucial to take a moment to acknowledge and celebrate our achievements and milestones. These moments of recognition serve as a source of motivation and help reinforce our success mindset. Celebrating our accomplishments reinforces the belief that we can achieve great things, fueling our motivation to strive for even greater success.

Celebrating achievements and milestones is not just about throwing a party or indulging in temporary pleasures. It is about taking the time to reflect on our progress and appreciate the efforts we have put in to reach our goals. Doing so creates a positive feedback loop in our mind, reinforcing the notion that hard work pays off and that we are on the right path.

One powerful way to celebrate achievements is by sharing them with others. By sharing our successes, we inspire those around us and solidify our belief in our capabilities. Whether in a formal setting, such as a presentation at work or informally with friends and family, sharing our achievements allows us to bask in the glory of our accomplishments and receive the recognition we deserve.

Another important aspect of celebrating achievements and milestones is setting new goals. While it is important to take a moment to relish our successes, it is equally important to keep pushing ourselves forward. By setting new goals, we ensure that our success journey continues and we avoid complacency. These new goals can be bigger and more ambitious than the ones we have already achieved, challenging us to unlock even more of our mind's full potential.

In conclusion, celebrating achievements and milestones is essential to a success mindset. By taking the time to acknowledge our progress, share our successes, and set new goals, we reinforce our belief in our capabilities and fuel our motivation to continue striving for success. So, let us embrace the power of celebration and use it to unlock our mind's full potential on the path to success.

Reflecting on Personal Growth

Personal growth is an essential aspect that cannot be overlooked in the journey toward success. We can unlock our mind's full potential through self-reflection and introspection and cultivate a success mindset. Reflecting on personal growth allows us to identify our strengths, weaknesses, and areas for improvement, enabling us to become the best version of ourselves.

One of the key elements of personal growth is self-awareness. Taking the time to reflect on our thoughts, emotions, and actions helps us understand ourselves better. By becoming aware of our patterns and behaviors, we can make conscious choices that align with our goals and values. Self-awareness also allows us to identify limiting beliefs or negative thought patterns that may be holding us back from reaching our full potential. We can challenge these beliefs through rejection and replace them with empowering and positive ones.

Another critical aspect of personal growth is learning from our experiences. Reflecting on our successes and failures allows us to gain valuable insights and lessons. It helps us analyze what worked and what didn't, enabling us to make better decisions in the future. By embracing a growth mindset, we can see setbacks as opportunities for growth and view failures as stepping stones toward success. Reflecting on our experiences also helps us celebrate our achievements and acknowledge our progress, boosting our confidence and motivation.

Furthermore, personal growth involves setting goals and continually striving for improvement. We can assess our progress toward our goals through rejection and make any necessary adjustments. It helps us stay focused, motivated, and accountable for our actions. Reflecting on personal growth also enables us to track our development over time, providing a sense of fulfillment and satisfaction as we witness our growth and transformation.

In conclusion, reflecting on personal growth is vital to cultivating a success mindset. It allows us to develop self-awareness, learn from our experiences, and set and achieve goals. Regularly reflecting on our journey can unlock our mind's full potential and continue to evolve and grow. Embracing personal growth leads to success and brings fulfillment and a sense of purpose to our lives. So, let us embark on this transformative journey of self-reflection and unlock our true potential.

Setting New Goals and Aspirations

One must constantly strive to set new goals and aspirations in the journey toward success. Adapting and evolving is crucial in unlocking your mind's full potential. Whether you are an aspiring entrepreneur, a professional seeking growth, or someone looking to elevate your life, setting new goals will guide you toward achieving your desired success.

The first step in setting new goals and aspirations is self-reflection. Take the time to understand your current situation, identify your strengths, and acknowledge areas for improvement. This introspection will help you determine what you truly want to achieve and give you a clear direction for setting your goals.

Once you have gained clarity about your aspirations, it is important to set SMART goals – Specific, Measurable, Achievable, Relevant, and Time-bound. Specific goals help you focus on what you want to accomplish, while measurable goals allow you to track your progress and stay motivated. Additionally, ensuring that your goals are achievable and relevant to your overall objectives will help you stay on the path to success. Lastly, setting your goals' deadlines will create a sense of urgency and provide a framework for your actions.

While setting new goals, it is essential to challenge yourself. Stepping out of your comfort zone and aiming for higher targets will push you to grow and develop a success mindset. Embrace the idea of taking calculated risks and be willing to learn from both successes and failures. Remember, every setback is an opportunity to grow and refine your goals and strategies.

To ensure you stay committed to your aspirations, it is crucial to create an action plan. Break down your goals into smaller, manageable tasks and create a timeline for completion. This approach will make your goals more attainable and help you focus on the necessary steps. Review and adjust your action plan to stay on track and maintain momentum.

Lastly, surround yourself with like-minded individuals who share your passion for success. Building a support network of people who inspire and motivate you will amplify your efforts and keep you accountable. Engage in discussions, seek advice, and celebrate each other's achievements along the way.

Setting new goals and aspirations is a continuous process. As you achieve one goal, setting new ones to keep progressing is essential. Embrace the journey, stay focused, and believe in your ability to unlock your mind's full potential. Success awaits those who dream big and take decisive action toward their goals.

Staying Committed to Continuous Improvement

In the journey toward success, one key factor that separates those who achieve greatness from those who don't is their commitment to continuous improvement. The path to success is not a one-time event but a lifelong growth and development process. This subchapter will explore the importance of staying committed to continuous improvement and how it can unlock your mind's full potential.

To begin, let's first understand the concept of continuous improvement. It refers to the ongoing effort to enhance one's skills, knowledge, and abilities with the aim of becoming better versions of ourselves. It involves a mindset that embraces change, seeks new challenges, and constantly strives for personal and professional growth.

One of the reasons why staying committed to continuous improvement is crucial is because it helps to cultivate a success mindset. By consistently seeking improvement, we train our minds to be open to new possibilities and opportunities. This mindset enables us to adapt to changing circumstances, overcome obstacles, and seize opportunities that come our way.

Moreover, continuous improvement allows us to stay ahead in an ever-evolving world. In today's fast-paced society, where technology and trends constantly change, individuals committed to continuous improvement gain a competitive edge. They are better equipped to adapt to new technologies, learn new skills, and stay relevant in their fields.

Personal fulfillment and satisfaction are other significant benefits of staying committed to continuous improvement. As humans, we have an innate desire to learn and grow. We experience a sense of accomplishment and fulfillment when we actively engage in self-improvement. This, in turn, boosts our self-confidence, motivation, and overall happiness.

However, staying committed to continuous improvement is not always easy. It requires discipline, persistence, and a willingness to step out of one's comfort zone. It may involve setting goals, seeking feedback, acquiring new knowledge, and developing new habits. It's important to remember that progress may not always be linear, and there may be setbacks along the way. But it is through these challenges that we learn, grow, and ultimately unlock our mind's full potential.

In conclusion, staying committed to continuous improvement is vital to developing a success mindset. It enables us to adapt, grow, and thrive in an ever-changing world. By embracing change, seeking new challenges, and consistently working towards self-improvement, we unlock our mind's full potential and pave the way for personal and professional success. So, let us commit ourselves to this lifelong journey of continuous improvement and embark on the path to success.

Inspiring Others and Paying It Forward

In our journey toward achieving success, we must recognize the power of inspiring others and paying it forward. As adults with a success mindset, we can positively impact the lives of those around us, creating a ripple effect of motivation and empowerment. This subchapter delves into the significance of inspiring others and how it can unlock our mind's full potential.

When we inspire others, we ignite a spark within them, encouraging them to believe in themselves and their abilities. Sharing our success stories demonstrates that ordinary individuals can accomplish extraordinary things. This motivates others to pursue their dreams and fosters a sense of community and support. When we inspire others, we contribute to a positive and empowering environment that uplifts everyone involved.

Furthermore, inspiring others is about sharing our successes and being vulnerable and transparent about our failures and obstacles. By opening up about the challenges we faced on our path to success, we show others that setbacks are not roadblocks but stepping stones. This mindset shift is crucial for individuals trying to develop a success mindset – the ability to view failures as opportunities for growth and learning.

Paying it forward is the natural progression of inspiring others. It involves sharing our knowledge, resources, and experiences to help others on their success journeys. We create a cycle of positivity and abundance by giving back to our communities and supporting those in need. The act of paying it forward not only benefits those we assist but also reinforces our success mindset. It reminds us that success is not solely about personal achievements but also about positively impacting the world.

In conclusion, inspiring others and paying it forward are integral to unlocking our mind's full potential and fostering a success mindset. As adults on the path to success, we have the power to inspire and uplift others, creating a supportive community that propels us all toward our goals. Sharing our successes, failures, and resources motivates others and strengthens our mindset and sense of purpose. Let us embrace the opportunity to inspire and pay it forward, knowing that our actions can change lives and contribute to a world filled with empowered individuals striving for success.

Thank you for reading!

Please log into our website to download your FREE worksheet.
https://koji.to/@Mindsuccess

Notes

Notes

Notes

Contact Us

Please contact us

www.mindyoursuccess86@gmail.com
https://koji.to/Mindsuccess

Printed in the USA
CPSIA information can be obtained
at www.ICGtesting.com
LVHW020826200823
755497LV00012B/533